More Wild Critters

Verse by Tim Jones • Photography by Tom Walker

GRAPHIC ARTS CENTER PUBLISHING™

For Mary Anne,
Justin,
Ariel,
& Eric

International Standard Book Number 1-55868-192-2
Library of Congress Catalog Number 94-75555
Verse © MCMXCIV by Tim Jones
Photographs © MCMXCIV by Tom Walker
Illustrations • Leslie Newman
Published by Graphic Arts Center Publishing Company
P.O. Box 10306 • Portland, Oregon 97210 • 503/226-2402
President • Charles M. Hopkins
Editor-in-Chief • Douglas A. Pfeiffer
Managing Editor • Jean Andrews
Production Manager • Richard L. Owsiany
Typographer • Harrison Typesetting, Inc.
Color Separations • Agency Litho
Printer • Moore Lithograph, Inc.
Bindery • Lincoln & Allen
Printed in the United States of America

TABLE OF CONTENTS

The New Wide Body

Puffin is a shy bird,
but today we almost caught her.
She ate too much and got too fat
to take off from the water.

With all her flaps a-flappin'
and runway length to spare,
she had too big a fuselage
to take off in the air.

4

Tufted puffin

Horned puffin

Greco-Roman marmots

6

Hoary marmots
love to play
in a rough
and tumble way.
If you think
this is a clash,
you should see
the tag-team match.

Marmots

Ducking the Breeze

A sailor's skill a goose applies
to find a lee for where he flies,
hidden from the breeze's whim
behind the Rocky Mountain Rim.

Canada Geese

Onward into the Shower

Will you come along, my dear?
We've schedules to keep.
But, please, my loving mother dear,
the water's much too deep.

Will you come along, my dear?
We're late to get our dinner.
But, please, my loving mother dear,
I'm not much of a swimmer.

Will you come along, my dear?
We're late, we've got to eat.
But, please, my loving mother dear,
the rocks feel slippery to my feet.

Will you come along, my dear?
We're going to get there last.
But, please, my loving mother dear,
the current's much too fast.

Will you come along, my dear,
and make the other side?
But, please, my loving mother dear,
all I do is slip and slide.

Will you come along, my dear?
We'll miss our dinner, yet.
But, please, my loving mother dear,
my belly's getting wet.

Will you come along, my dear?
An appointment we've to keep.
You've always told me, mother dear,
don't get in too deep.

Will you come along, my dear?
Deep is where to be.
You tricked me, Mom, and now I see;
Your path is just a bath for me.

Rocky Mountain elk

But Think of
All the Starving Mice in . . .

I don't like to eat my veggies,
carrots, greens, and 'taters.
I hide them in my whiskers,
so I can dump them later.

12

Collared pika

Bobcat Just Went Splat

Felis rufus,
What a doofus,
He always jumps with grace.

Felis rufus,
What a doofus,
He landed on his face.

Felis rufus,
What a doofus,
In jumps he shows no fear.

Felis rufus,
What a doofus,
He landed on his ear.

14

Bobcat (Felus rufus)

You'll Believe a Cat Can Fly

If I could fly, I'd tell my Mom,
and, know what she would say?
She'd say, "You know a cat can't fly.
Now leave me be and go away."

If I could fly, I'd tell my Mom
I'd been across the ridge.
She'd say, "You know a cat can't fly.
Now let me sleep a smidge."

If I could fly, I'd tell my Mom
I'd crossed the mountain pass.
She'd say, "You know a cat can't fly.
Now let me lie here in the grass."

If I could fly, I'd tell my Mom
I'd flown across the moon.
She'd say, "You know a cat can't fly.
Now let me sleep 'til noon."

I don't care if Mom believes
I fly across the sand.
Believe or not, she'd best watch out —
I need a place to land!

16

Mountain lion cub and mother

Formal Dining, Red Tie

A black-necked stilt went out to dine
along the ocean shore.
He put on evening wear of black,
and legs of red he wore.

Black-necked stilt

So, too, did Oystercatcher
travel to the beach,
and brought along his beak of red,
his food with which to reach.

Why would these birds so different,
dining in the coastal venue,
both be wearing red
as they looked about the menu?

Of course, then, when they chose
the thing on which they fed,
the silly thing so foolishly
came swimming toward the red.

Oystercatcher

Critters in the Garden

When I go walking in the woods,
I never see a thing.
I never see an animal
on hoof or paw or wing.

There are some big ones out there;
that I know for fact.
So how can something
big as deer, even hide its rack?

I guess I'll just keep walking,
ever on my guard.
Someday I hope I'll see
some kind of critter in my yard.

Mule deer with antlers

Don't Fence Me In

Ram be nimble.
Ram jump higher.
Ram's got to clear
the man's barbed wire.

Montana Bighorn

The DOE Line

People on this earth
once were more afraid.
They had an early warning line
'case someone sent some bad their way.

Called DEW line for short,
it helped allay their fears,
like the big-eared D.O.E. line
warns the Rocky Mountain deer.

Six-month-old mule deer

A Stucky Stituation

There's lots of things can stick you,
Devil's club and rosebush spine.
There's lots of things can trick you,
even some you might not mind.

There's lots of things can nick you,
like briars on a berry vine.
Can anything funnier prick you
than a porcupine's behind?

Porcupine

Motown Moose

A moose went out to boogie at night.
He dressed himself to look just right.
He donned his very finest thread,
wearin' a twig hat on his head.

Moose

A Meal at the Hard Rock Cafe

Mom took Kid to eat one day
upon a meal of stone.
Said Kid, "There is no meat in here.
This thing is only bone."

Still . . .
It filled the goats' propensity
for eating things of density.

But then . . .
It rearranged their dentistry.

Mountain goat nanny and kid

Lambsprings

High up in the mountains,
nothing grows too tall.
Sometimes in the high rocks,
nothing grows at all.

So, when we're doing lambsprings
and playing with each other,
with nothing else to jump,
I have to jump my brother.

Two-week-old Dall sheep lambs

The Champ Can Lick 'em All

Brown bear on the coastline,
grizzly on the mountain tall;
he's the baddest animal,
the baddest one of all.
The others give him lots of room,
'cause he can lick 'em all.

Grizzly bear

No Autographs, Please

I find myself a symbol
of a nation great to see,
a bird of great distinction
and great celebrity.

But like so many birds of fame,
I'd like some privacy.
So, when my fans arrive in flocks,
I'd really like to flee.

Bald eagles

A Walrus Kind of Shade

Walrus in the daytime
sleeping in the light.
Walrus in the daytime
in the sun so bright.
All he's got's a flipper
to make himself some night.

Walrus

And, No Substitutions

The game was so much fun
they all tried to play.
They tripped on one another
and they got in the way.

Then, when all the players
went back to the huddle,
they found they had too many
ducks there for the puddle.

So what can all those ducks do
When it's water that they lack,
But mill about and bump around
And quack and quack and quack?

Mallards

Put On a Happy Face

We have to keep in mind,
when things are out of place,
that things we do not know about
can show a gruesome face.

But put them where they fit,
and if they aren't misplaced,
you know a face this ugly
to another moose looks snuggly.

Moose

Watch That Diet

The thing about hares is this:
They can't read.
And this: They eat
everything in their sight.
So pity the bunny
who thought it was funny
to eat himself into a fright.

DANGER

Snowshoe hare

With Apologies to Mother Goose

Wood duck

Hi diddle dee, the duck's in the tree;

The stream washed away the raccoon;

Raccoon

Harp seal

The seal rolled over to see such a sport,

And the bird hit his head on the moon.

Bald eagle

More Wild Critter Facts

BALD EAGLE: At one time the bald eagle was almost extinct in the contiguous 48 states. Not bald at all, they have white head feathers. It takes an eagle up to five years to grow the white head and tail feathers.

BLACK-NECKED STILT: This wading bird feeds on invertebrates and soft shelled critters at the margins of lakes and oceans. Its legs are the longest for its body size in the world of wading birds.

BLACK OYSTERCATCHER: Another wading bird, the oystercatcher stalks shorelines searching for mollusks and invertebrates. Its colored bill may attract prey.

BOBCAT *(Felis rufus):* These large cousins of the common house cat feed mostly on small birds and rodents. Mice are the principal element in most bobcat diets.

CANADA GEESE: Geese migrate long distances from their winter range in the southern United States to nesting grounds in the far north of Canada and Alaska. Canada geese mate for life.

DALL SHEEP: Cousins to the Rocky Mountain bighorn sheep, these all-white sheep live in Alaska, the Yukon, British Columbia, and the Northwest Territories. Their white coats are camouflage in winter from predators, but also protection from the sun in summer on the high alpine slopes.

GRIZZLY BEAR: Grizzly bears usually are more afraid of people than people are afraid of them. In Alaska, grizzlies can hibernate for up to nine months each year. Most bears live on grass and other vegetation.

HARP SEAL: Pups are born white on ice in early spring, and—as ice melts in late spring—are abandoned by their mothers. In time, they enter the water, knowing instinctively how to swim and fend for themselves.

HOARY MARMOTS: They may hibernate for as long as nine months in a burrow they share with others in their extended family.

HORNED PUFFIN: Called sea parrots by old-time sailors, puffins feed from the ocean and nest in burrows on rocky cliffs.

MALLARD: The mallard is the most numerous of all waterfowl. The drake has a bright green head and neck; the hens are drab brown. They are dabbling feeders, meaning they "tip up" rather than dive for their food.

MOOSE: These giant deer can weigh up to 1,500 pounds. Moose lose their antlers in December and grow them again in the spring. They often feed on plants in lakes, ducking under to reach their dinner.

MOUNTAIN LION: These large cats feed mostly on deer. They are secretive and rarely seen; however, in recent years, local populations have increased near cities and towns.

MULE DEER: Large ears give this western deer remarkable hearing. Fawns are born with spotted coats in the spring, but by fall they have lost their spots, and their color matches that of the adults. Each fall the males shed their antlers, which they grow again in the spring.

PACIFIC WALRUS: They live in the Bering Sea and their scientific name means "tooth walker." They use their tusks to pull themselves up onto ice or rocky shores. They eat mollusks that they locate on the ocean floor, using their sensitive whiskers.

PIKA: Pikas also are known as "hay makers" because in late summer and early fall they cut grasses to dry for winter, piling the plants into "hay stacks."

PORCUPINE: They eat the bark of evergreen trees, in some cases killing the tree. They also are attracted to salt-encrusted wood products and have been known to chew ax handles and canoe paddles seeking the salt left by sweaty hands.

RACCOON: Raccoons sometimes live near water, and they have a habit of "washing" their food before they eat. They don't really wash their food, but it appears the wetting helps them swallow.

ROCKY MOUNTAIN BIGHORN SHEEP: Both rams and ewes have horns, which they keep and grow all of their lives. The ewe has small, sharp-pointed horns, while the ram has horns that may grow almost into a circle.

ROCKY MOUNTAIN ELK: Elk were once plains animals that shared grasslands with bison and antelope. As humans took over the prairies for ranching and farming, elk were restricted mainly to the mountains.

ROCKY MOUNTAIN GOAT: The Rocky Mountain goat has suction-cup-like hooves that enable it to walk on the steepest cliffs. More sure-footed even than mountain sheep, the goat has few natural enemies. Their warm, woolly coat protects them from the cold of winter.

SNOWSHOE HARE: Hares turn white in the winter, brown in the summer. They have long hind legs and wide paws that allow them to run across the top of deep snow.

TUFTED PUFFIN: Puffins shed their colorful bills each year. They reach their rich color only in the spring breeding season.

WOOD DUCK: The wood duck is one of only a few kinds of ducks that nest in trees.